NOV - - 2013

Y0-BZH-030

21st Century
Basic Skills
Library

SHAPES EVERYWHERE!

by Cecilia Minden, PhD

Cherry Lake Publishing • Ann Arbor, Michigan

Published in the United States of America
by Cherry Lake Publishing
Ann Arbor, Michigan
www.cherrylakepublishing.com

Photo Credits: Cover and page 1, ©iStockphoto.com/ferrantraite;
page 6, ©iStockphoto.com/Zoediak; pages 8 and 18, ©iStockphoto.
com/NinaMalyna; pages 10 and 18, ©Phil Syme/Shutterstock, Inc.;
page 12, ©L. Kragt Bakker/Shutterstock, Inc.; pages 14 and 18, ©Alegria/
Shutterstock, Inc.; page 20, ©iStockphoto.com/Petegar

Copyright ©2011 by Cherry Lake Publishing
All rights reserved. No part of this book may be reproduced or utilized in
any form or by any means without written permission from the publisher.

Library of Congress Cataloging-in-Publication Data
Minden, Cecilia.
  Shapes everywhere/by Cecilia Minden.
      p. cm.—(21st century basic skills library. Level 1)
  Includes bibliographical references and index.
  ISBN-13: 978-1-60279-850-2 (lib. bdg.)
  ISBN-10: 1-60279-850-8 (lib. bdg.)
  1. Shapes—Juvenile literature. 2. Geometry—Juvenile literature.
I. Title. II. Series.
  QA445.5.M56 2010
  516'.15—dc22   2009048569

Cherry Lake Publishing would like to acknowledge
the work of The Partnership for 21st Century Skills.
Please visit www.21stcenturyskills.org for more information.

Printed in the United States of America
Corporate Graphics Inc.
July 2010
CLFA07

TABLE OF CONTENTS

Circles and Spheres

A circle is round.

Which shape is a circle?

A **sphere** is round, too.

Which ball is a sphere?

8

Squares and Cubes

A **square** has four sides.

Each side is the same size.

Which one is a square?

A **cube** has a square on each side.

How many cubes do you see?

Triangles and Cones

A **triangle** has three sides.

Which shape is a triangle?

A **cone** has a circle on one end.

It has a **point** on the other end.

Which treat is in a cone?

2-D Shapes

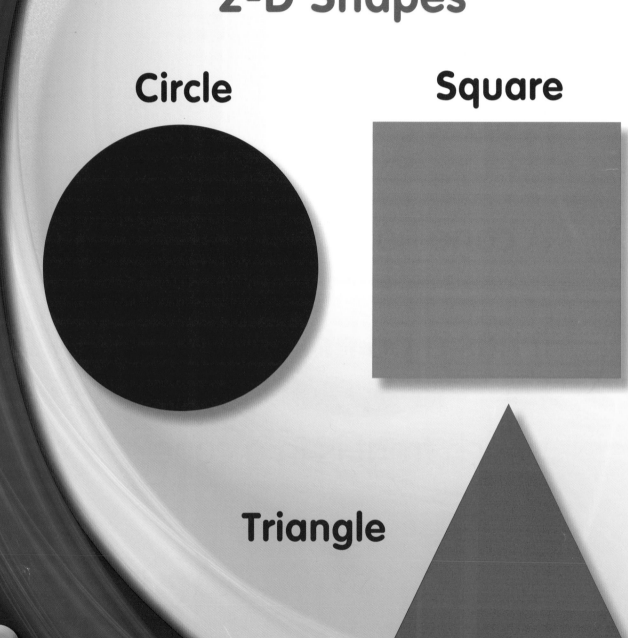

Circle

Square

Triangle

Some shapes are tall and wide.

They are 2-D shapes.

3-D Shapes

Cone

Sphere

Cube

Some shapes are tall, wide, and deep.

They are 3-D shapes.

Look around!

What shapes do you see?

Find Out More

BOOK

Rissman, Rebecca. *Shapes in Sports*. Chicago: Heinemann Library, 2009.

WEB SITE

Shapes at EnchantedLearning.com
www.enchantedlearning.com/themes/shapes.shtml
Learn about shapes with games and crafts.

Glossary

cone (KOHN) 3-D shape that has a circle on one end and a point on the other end

cube (KYOOB) a 3-D shape with six square faces

point (POYNT) the sharp end of something

sphere (SFEER) a 3-D round ball or globe shape

square (SKWAIR) a 2-D shape with four straight sides that are all the same length

triangle (TRYE-ang-guhl) a 2-D shape with three straight sides

Home and School Connection

Use this list of words from the book to help your child become a better reader. Word games and writing activities can help beginning readers reinforce literacy skills.

2-D	do	point	tall
3-D	each	round	the
a	end	same	they
and	four	see	three
are	has	shape	too
around	how	shapes	treat
ball	in	side	triangle
circle	is	sides	triangles
circles	it	size	what
cone	look	some	which
cones	many	sphere	wide
cube	on	spheres	you
cubes	one	square	
deep	other	squares	

Index

About the Author

Cecilia Minden is the former Director of the Language and Literacy Program at the Harvard Graduate School of Education. She currently works as a literacy consultant for school and library publishers and is the author of more than 100 books for children.